POSTWAR AMERICA
THE VIETNAM WAR

by Nick Rebman

FOCUS READERS
NAVIGATOR

WWW.FOCUSREADERS.COM

Copyright © 2024 by Focus Readers®, Mendota Heights, MN 55120. All rights reserved. No part of this book may be reproduced or utilized in any form or by any means without written permission from the publisher.

Focus Readers is distributed by North Star Editions: sales@northstareditions.com | 888-417-0195

Produced for Focus Readers by Red Line Editorial.

Content Consultant: Ronald Frankum, PhD, Professor of History, Millersville University

Photographs ©: Horst Faas/AP Images, cover, 1, 8; AP Images, 4–5, 15, 17, 21, 27, 29; Shutterstock Images, 7; Department of Defense/AP Images, 10–11; Pictures From History/Newscom, 12; Oliver Noonan/AP Images, 18–19; Frances Starner/AP Images, 23; Rick Merron/AP Images, 24–25

Library of Congress Cataloging-in-Publication Data
Names: Rebman, Nick, author.
Title: The Vietnam War / by Nick Rebman.
Description: Mendota Heights, MN : Focus Readers, [2024] | Series: Postwar America | Includes bibliographical references and index. | Audience: Grades 4-6
Identifiers: LCCN 2023036580 (print) | LCCN 2023036581 (ebook) | ISBN 9798889980445 (hardcover) | ISBN 9798889980872 (paperback) | ISBN 9798889981688 (pdf) | ISBN 9798889981305 (ebook)
Subjects: LCSH: Vietnam War, 1961-1975--Juvenile literature. | Vietnam War, 1961-1975--United States--Juvenile literature.
Classification: LCC DS557.7 .R474 2024 (print) | LCC DS557.7 (ebook) | DDC 959.704/3--dc23/eng/20230803
LC record available at https://lccn.loc.gov/2023036580
LC ebook record available at https://lccn.loc.gov/2023036581

Printed in the United States of America
Mankato, MN
012024

ABOUT THE AUTHOR

Nick Rebman is a writer and editor who lives in Minnesota.

TABLE OF CONTENTS

CHAPTER 1
The Path to War 5

CHAPTER 2
The War Expands 11

VOICES FROM THE PAST
War Crimes 16

CHAPTER 3
Communist Victory 19

CHAPTER 4
Legacy of the War 25

Focus on the Vietnam War • 30
Glossary • 31
To Learn More • 32
Index • 32

CHAPTER 1

THE PATH TO WAR

In the mid-1800s, France set up **colonies** in Southeast Asia. However, many local people wanted to be **independent**. In 1946, a war broke out. And in 1954, Vietnamese soldiers defeated the French. The peace agreement said France had to give up its colonies. It also said Vietnam would be divided in half for two years.

President Ho Chi Minh led Vietnam to victory over France in 1954. The French army received support from the United States.

North Vietnam set up a **Communist** government. Its leaders had close ties to other Communist countries. South Vietnam's government opposed Communism. Its leaders relied heavily on US support.

Vietnam was supposed to be reunited in 1956. At that time, an election would take place. People would choose a new leader. However, a Communist was most likely to win. South Vietnam's leaders did not want that to happen. They had not signed the peace agreement in 1954. So, they refused to hold the election.

Some people in South Vietnam supported Communism. By 1960, they had formed an army called the Viet Cong. They started attacking South Vietnam's army and government officials. North Vietnam gave the Viet Cong orders. Their goal was to take over South Vietnam.

NORTH AND SOUTH VIETNAM, 1954

 US military advisors helped train villagers to resist Viet Cong attacks.

North Vietnam and the Viet Cong were not a direct threat to the United States. But US leaders did not want Communism to spread. So, the United States sent military advisors. They trained South Vietnam's army.

In 1964, two US ships said they were attacked by North Vietnam. The reports were not fully true. Even so, the US Congress took action. It gave new powers to President Lyndon B. Johnson. He could now use military force in Southeast Asia. He didn't need to wait for Congress to declare war.

THE COLD WAR

The Cold War (1947–1991) was a conflict between the Soviet Union and the United States. The Soviet Union wanted Communism to spread. The United States wanted to stop it. The Soviet Union and the United States never fought directly. But they helped different sides in several wars. The Vietnam War was one example.

CHAPTER 2
THE WAR EXPANDS

South Vietnam received heavy support from the United States. Yet South Vietnam's army struggled against the Viet Cong. President Johnson decided to take further action. He ordered US planes to bomb North Vietnam.

Tens of thousands of **civilians** were killed. But the Viet Cong soldiers in South

The United States dropped nearly 8 million tons (nearly 7 million metric tons) of bombs during the Vietnam War.

 The Viet Cong used a system of paths through Laos and Cambodia to move supplies into South Vietnam.

Vietnam kept fighting. These soldiers hoped to spread fear. They used torture, kidnapping, and murder. They wanted to show that South Vietnam's government could not keep people safe.

The Viet Cong used brutal methods. Still, Communism appealed to many people in Vietnam. Most people in the country were poor. Only a small number were wealthy. But the wealthy people held power. They made rules that kept everyone else poor. Communist leaders promised that everyone would be equal. That gave many people a strong reason to keep fighting.

Also, many people in Vietnam did not want foreign powers in their country. That included US soldiers. They believed the US soldiers were no different from the earlier French invaders.

By 1965, South Vietnam's army seemed ready to lose. So, President Johnson sent ground forces to Vietnam.

By the end of 1966, more than 350,000 US soldiers were there.

US soldiers searched for Viet Cong bases. However, it was hard to know who was a Viet Cong soldier and who was a civilian. As a result, US forces killed many civilians. They also caused massive destruction. Their actions did not bring victory, though. That's because US soldiers left the area after each battle. Communist fighters returned later.

In early 1968, North Vietnam launched the Tet Offensive. Communist soldiers carried out more than 100 attacks. The attacks were not successful. But they had a major effect on the opinions of

Attacks from both sides caused damage to civilians throughout Vietnam.

US citizens. People saw the fighting on TV. Some thought it was wrong. Some were worried for US troops. Over time, that led to a drop in support for the war.

VOICES FROM THE PAST

WAR CRIMES

On March 16, 1968, US soldiers killed hundreds of unarmed civilians. The victims included men, women, children, and babies. The event became known as the My Lai Massacre. It was one of the many **war crimes** that were committed during the Vietnam War.

Vo Cao Loi was 16 years old at the time. "All I could hear were explosions," he said. "The ground was shaking."[1] Loi survived the massacre. But US soldiers killed 18 of his relatives. Loi later joined the Viet Cong. He wanted to fight back against the United States.

Viet Cong soldiers also committed war crimes. In 1967, they murdered hundreds in Dak Son. In early 1968, they killed many civilians in the city of Hue. Nguyen Cong Minh's father was one victim.

Civilians cover victims' bodies after the Dak Son massacre. Viet Cong soldiers attacked with flamethrowers and guns.

She said many people were "tied up with their hands behind their backs." After that, they "were all buried alive."[2] Brutal actions such as these happened throughout the war.

1. James Pearson and Minh Nguyen. "Survivors of Vietnam's My Lai massacre remember 'darkness and silence.'" *Reuters*. Reuters, 15 Mar. 2018. Web. 20 Apr. 2023.
2. "Vietnam: A Television History; Tet, 1968; Interview with Mrs. Nguyen Cong Minh." *Open Vault*. WGBH Educational Foundation, n.d. Web. 20 Apr. 2023.

CHAPTER 3

COMMUNIST VICTORY

In early 1969, Richard Nixon became the new US president. Nixon didn't think the United States could win the war. But he did not want to pull US soldiers out of Vietnam quickly. He worried it would make the United States look weak. Instead, Nixon wanted to reach a peace agreement with North Vietnam.

Many civilians were left homeless due to bombings.

Meanwhile, both sides continued to fight. People continued to die. Nixon also ordered air attacks in Cambodia and Laos. These neighboring countries were **neutral**. However, the Viet Cong was hiding soldiers and supplies there.

The American public learned about the attacks. Many people were angry that the

PROTEST MOVEMENT

Millions of Americans opposed the war in Vietnam. Some people went to classes taught by anti-war leaders. Others spoke out against companies that made weapons for the US military. And some people marched in the streets. They demanded that the president pull US soldiers out of Vietnam. Protests happened at more than 1,300 colleges around the country.

In November 1969, hundreds of thousands of people attended an anti-war march in Washington, DC.

war was expanding. The war became even less popular in the United States.

By April 1969, more than 500,000 US soldiers were in Vietnam. In June, Nixon said he would reduce US forces. South Vietnam would start leading the fight. But this process would be slow. The US military would still need many soldiers there.

In December 1969, the United States began a **draft lottery**. Most of the Americans who were sent to Vietnam came from poorer families. Wealthy families often found ways to avoid the draft.

In 1972, North Vietnam launched a full invasion of the South. US forces helped fight against it. North Vietnam's leaders realized they could not win a quick victory. So, they agreed to peace talks. In January 1973, the two sides signed a treaty.

After North Vietnam took control, Saigon was renamed Ho Chi Minh City.

US soldiers left Vietnam. Yet the fighting continued. In April 1975, North Vietnam's army took control of Saigon. This city was the capital of South Vietnam. The Communist forces had won the war. All of Vietnam was under their control.

CHAPTER 4

LEGACY OF THE WAR

Historians do not know exactly how many people died in the Vietnam War. Up to two million civilians were killed. More than one million Viet Cong and North Vietnamese soldiers died. So did at least 200,000 South Vietnamese soldiers. More than 58,000 US soldiers were also killed.

Millions of civilians were injured during the war.

In addition, much of Vietnam was destroyed. Cities, farms, and forests lay in ruins. Millions of people lost their homes. Many people starved.

The US military also left behind thousands of unexploded bombs. These bombs often lay buried in fields or

AGENT ORANGE

Agent Orange is a chemical that kills plants. The US military sprayed it over much of Vietnam. Military leaders had two goals. First, they wanted to destroy forests where the Viet Cong hid. Second, they wanted to destroy crops that could feed the Viet Cong. Agent Orange caused horrible damage to Vietnam's environment. It also caused serious health problems for millions of people.

It took years to rebuild after the war's destruction.

forests. Many are still active. Every year, old bombs are set off accidentally. They have killed more than 40,000 people since the war ended. At least 60,000 others have been injured. The victims are often farmers and children.

27

Many people in Vietnam fought against the Communists during the war. Some of them fled the country in 1975. But others could not leave. The Communist government often **oppressed** these people. Many were tortured and starved. They were also forced to do hard labor.

Millions of **refugees** left Vietnam, too. They often traveled on crowded, unsafe boats. Up to 400,000 people died at sea. Survivors went to refugee camps in nearby countries. They lived in awful conditions.

Soon, the nearby countries could not handle the huge number of people. Western countries agreed to take in many

Refugees on boats faced terrible conditions. Approximately one-third died on the journey.

refugees. More than one million people settled in the United States. But their lives were often difficult. Many Americans did not welcome them. For them and many others, the effects of the Vietnam War are still felt.

FOCUS ON
THE VIETNAM WAR

Write your answers on a separate piece of paper.

1. Write a paragraph explaining the causes of the Vietnam War.

2. Do you think the United States should have fought the Vietnam War? Why or why not?

3. When did the United States begin a draft lottery for the Vietnam War?
    - **A.** 1954
    - **B.** 1969
    - **C.** 1975

4. Why did Viet Cong soldiers fight against South Vietnam's government?
    - **A.** They wanted to make sure the war didn't expand into Cambodia and Laos.
    - **B.** They wanted to unite Vietnam under Communist rule.
    - **C.** They wanted to destroy Communist bases in Vietnam's jungles.

Answer key on page 32.

GLOSSARY

civilians
People who are not in the military.

colonies
Areas controlled by a country that is far away.

Communist
Having to do with a political idea that calls for all property to be owned by the public.

draft lottery
A system that randomly chooses people to serve in the military.

independent
Able to make decisions without being controlled by another government.

neutral
Not supporting either side in a disagreement.

oppressed
Treated someone in a way that was unjust and unfair.

refugees
People forced to leave their homes due to war or disaster.

war crimes
Serious crimes committed during a war, such as killing civilians or torturing prisoners.

TO LEARN MORE

BOOKS

Gunderson, Megan M. *Lyndon B. Johnson*. Minneapolis: Abdo Publishing, 2021.

Kenney, Karen Latchana. *TV Brings Battle into the Home with the Vietnam War*. North Mankato, MN: Capstone Press, 2019.

Loh-Hagan, Virginia. *Southeast Asian Refugee Resettlement in the U.S.* Ann Arbor, MI: Cherry Lake Publishing Group, 2023.

NOTE TO EDUCATORS

Visit **www.focusreaders.com** to find lesson plans, activities, links, and other resources related to this title.

INDEX

Agent Orange, 26

bombs, 11, 26–27

civilians, 11, 14, 16, 25
Cold War, 9
Communism, 6, 8–9, 12–14, 23, 28

Dak Son, 16–17
draft, 22

France, 5, 13

Johnson, Lyndon B., 9, 11, 13

My Lai Massacre, 16

Nixon, Richard, 19–21

protests, 20

refugees, 28–29

Saigon, 23

Tet Offensive, 14

Viet Cong, 7–8, 11–12, 14, 16, 20, 25–26

war crimes, 16–17

Answer Key: 1. Answers will vary; 2. Answers will vary; 3. B; 4. B

32